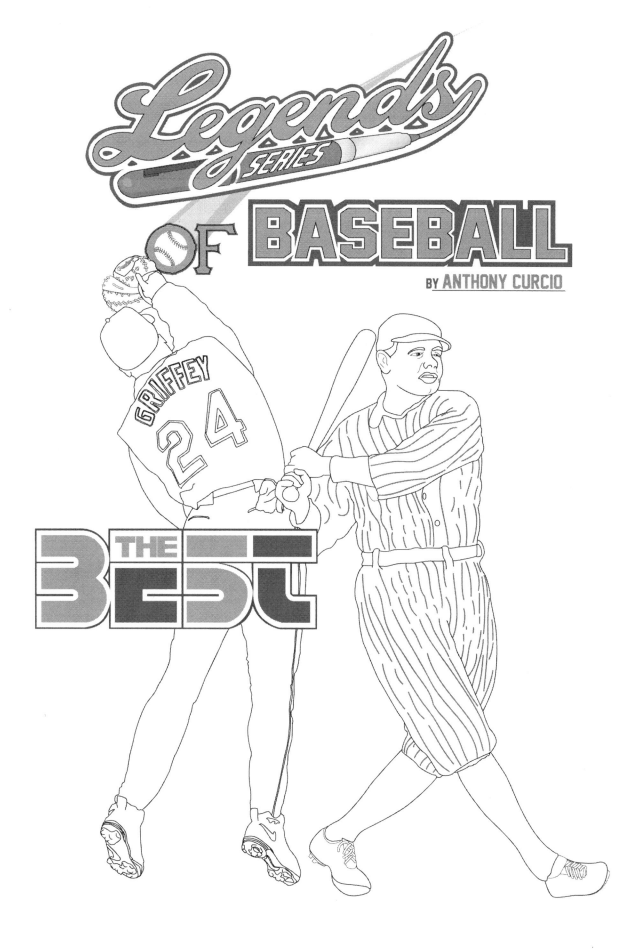

KEY LEGEND

ERA	Earned Run Average		AL	American League		RBI leader	Runs Batted In
SO	Strikeouts		NL	National League		Batting Champ	Leader in batting average
Cy Young	Top pitching award		MVP	Most Valuable Player		Silver Slugger	Given to best player at each
Triple Crown	Leage leader in Wins, ERA		ROY	Rookie of the Year			position in both AL and NL.
	and strikeouts in 1 season.		W.S.	World Series		Triple Crown	League leader in BA, home
							runs and RBI.

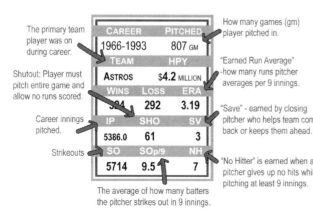

The primary team player was on during career.

How many games (gm) player pitched in.

Length of player's career. First game - Last Game.

"Highest Paid Year": most money player made in any 1-year period.

"Earned Run Average" -how many runs pitcher averages per 9 innings.

Shutout: Player must pitch entire game and allow no runs scored.

At Bats: How many times a player was up to bat.

"Batting Average": how many hits the player averages per 'at bat.' (hits / at bats = BA)

"Save" - earned by closing pitcher who helps team come back or keeps them ahead.

Career innings pitched.

Home Runs

"Runs Batted In": How many runs score because of player hit.

Strikeouts

"No Hitter" is earned when a pitcher gives up no hits while pitching at least 9 innings.

Stolen Bases

"ERR" = Error: Players mistake that allows other team to advance bases.

The average of how many batters the pitcher strikes out in 9 innings.

CAREER	PITCHED		CAREER	GAMES
1966-1993	807 GM		1986-2007	2986
TEAM	HPY		TEAM	HPY
ASTROS	$4.2 MILLION		GIANTS	$22 MILLION
WINS	LOSS	ERA	AB	HITS	BA
324	292	3.19	9847	2935	.298
IP	SHO	SV	HR	RUNS	RBI
5386.0	61	3	762	2227	1996
SO	SOp/9	NH	SB	SO	ERR
5714	9.5	7	514	1539	97

1B

ALBERTPUJOLS

BEST SEASON STATS

2003	AVG	HR	RBI
	.359	43	124

CAREER	GAMES	
2001-2017	2454	
TEAM	**HPY**	
CARDINALS	$26 MILLION	
AB	**HITS**	**BA**
9252	2853	.308
HR	**RUNS**	**RBI**
594	1679	1840
SB	**SO**	**ERR**
108	1078	99

THE BEST

Albert Pujols (b. 1980) was born and raised in the Dominican Republic. He was very poor as a child and practiced baseball with a lime as a ball and a milk carton for a glove. When he was 16 years old, he and his family moved to the U.S. and Albert went to high school in Missouri. In high school, he was twice named All-State and hit a 450 foot home run! 402nd pick in the 1999 MLB Draft, but named Rookie of the Year! 10x All-Star, 3x NL MVP, 2x home run leader, 6x Silver Slugger, 2x Gold Glove, 2x W.S. Champ!

SS

ALEX RODRIGUEZ

BEST SEASON STATS

2007	AVG	HR	RBI
	.314	54	156

CAREER	GAMES	
1994-2016	2784	
TEAM	**HPY**	
YANKEES	$33 MILLION	
AB	**HITS**	**BA**
10566	3115	.295
HR	**RUNS**	**RBI**
696	2021	2086
SB	**SO**	**ERR**
329	2287	131

THE BEST

Alex Rodriquez (b. 1975) was born in New York but moved with his parents to the Dominican Republic when he was 4 years old. They later returned to the U.S. and Alex went to high school in Miami, Florida where he was a standout in baseball and football. 1st overall pick in 1993 MLB Draft by the Seattle Mariners. "A-Rod" was a 14-time All-Star selection, a 3x AL MVP, 2x Gold Glove Award winner, 10x Silver Slugger, 5x AL home run leader, 2x MLB RBI leader, MLB batting champ, and World Series Champ ('09).

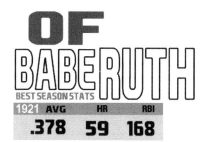

OF BABE RUTH
BEST SEASON STATS

1921	AVG	HR	RBI
	.378	59	168

CAREER		GAMES
1914-1935		2503
TEAM		HPY
YANKEES		$80 THOUSAND
AB	HITS	BA
8399	2873	.342
HR	RUNS	RBI
714	2174	2214
SB	SO	ERR
123	1330	155

George Herman "Babe" Ruth (1895-1948) was born and raised in Maryland. When he was 7 years old he was sent to a reformatory school/orphanage. In his free time, he and the other boys would play baseball. The "Babe" took to the game quickly and his legend began to grow, not just as a great hitter but also as a pitcher. He went pro in 1914 and eventually became the most famous to ever play the game. All-Star, *7x World Series champ*, AL MVP, Batting Champ, *12x home-run leader*, 6x RBI leader. The list goes on...

LF
BARRY BONDS

BEST SEASON STATS

2001	AVG	HR	RBI
	.328	73	137

CAREER		GAMES
1986-2007		2986
TEAM		HPY
GIANTS		$22 MILLION
AB	HITS	BA
9847	2935	.298
HR	RUNS	RBI
762	2227	1996
SB	SO	ERR
514	1539	97

Barry Bonds (b.1964) was born and raised in California. His dad, Bobby Bonds, also played professional baseball (also primarily with the Giants). In high school Barry excelled in baseball, basketball and football. He received All-American honors his senior year, batting .467. He turned down a $70,000 signing bonus to go pro and went to Arizona State University to play instead. Drafted 6th overall in 1985 by Pirates. 14x All-Star, *7x NL MVP*, 8x Gold Glove, 12x Silver Slugger, 2x batting champ, 2x home run leader.

P
BOB GIBSON

BEST SEASON STATS

1968	W-L	ERA	SO	SO P/9
	22 - 9	1.12	268	7.9

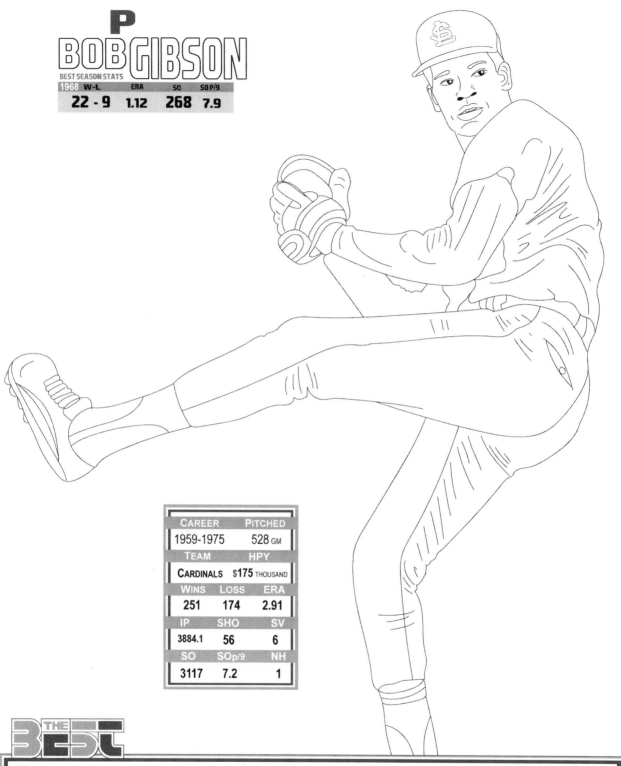

CAREER	PITCHED	
1959-1975	528 GM	
TEAM	**HPY**	
CARDINALS	$175 THOUSAND	
WINS	**LOSS**	**ERA**
251	174	2.91
IP	**SHO**	**SV**
3884.1	56	6
SO	**SOp/9**	**NH**
3117	7.2	1

Bob Gibson (b. 1935) was born and raised in Nebraska. He had 6 brothers and sisters. He played baseball and basketball growing up and was on several teams, many that his oldest brother coached. From a baby through his high school years, Gibson faced many illnesses that he managed to overcome. He earned a scholarship to play basketball at Creighton University where he became an All-American. 9x All-Star, 2x W.S. Champ, NL MVP (1968), 2x Cy Young, 2x W.S. MVP, 9x Gold Glove, wins, ERA and strikeout leader.

3B
BROOKS ROBINSON

BEST SEASON STATS

1964	AVG	HR	RBI
	.317	28	118

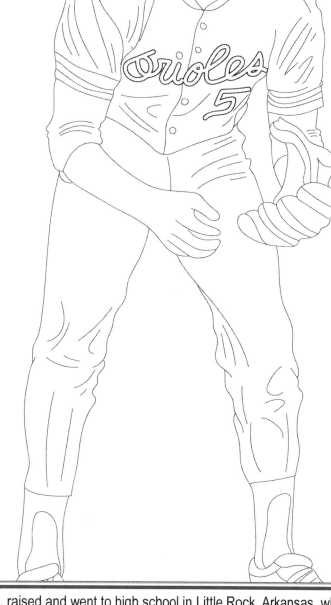

CAREER	GAMES	
1955-1977	2896	

TEAM	HPY	
ORIOLES	$120 THOUSAND	

AB	HITS	BA
10654	2848	.267

HR	RUNS	RBI
268	1232	1357

SB	SO	ERR
28	990	263

Brooks Robinson (b. 1937) was born, raised and went to high school in Little Rock, Arkansas, where he was scouted by the Razorbacks program but was drafted by the U.S. Army. Brooks was later signed by the Orioles as a free agent in 1955. He went on to play his entire 23-year career for the Baltimore Orioles. Considered one of the greatest defensive 3rd baseman ever, nicknamed "Mr. Hoover" (after the vacuum!). 18x All-Star, 2x World Series Champ, AL MVP ('70), *16x Gold Glove*, RBI leader ('64), All-Century Team.

SS/3B
CAL RIPKEN JR.

BEST SEASON STATS

1991	AVG	HR	RBI
	.323	34	114

CAREER	GAMES	
1981-2001	3001	
TEAM	HPY	
ORIOLES	$6.8 MILLION	
AB	HITS	BA
11551	3184	.276
HR	RUNS	RBI
431	1647	1695
SB	SO	ERR
36	1305	225

THE BEST

Cal Ripken Jr. (b. 1960) was born and raised in Maryland, however spent most of his younger years traveling with his family - as his dad, Cal Ripken Sr. was a former MLB player and Coach for the Baltimore Orioles - where Ripken Jr. would spend his entire career. The 48th overall pick in the 1978 Major League Draft. One of the best all-around shortstops of all time. 19x All-Star selections, World Series Champ ('83), 2x AL MVP, Rookie of the Year ('82), 2x Gold Glove, 8x Silver Slugger, MLB Record 2,632 straight games!

P
CHRISTY MATHEWSON

BEST SEASON STATS

1905	W-L	ERA	SO	SO P/9
	31 - 9	1.28	206	5.5

CAREER		PITCHED
1900-1916		636 GM
TEAM		HPY
GIANTS (mets)		$10 THOUSAND
WINS	LOSS	ERA
373	188	2.13
IP	SHO	SV
4788.2	79	30
SO	SOp/9	NH
2507	4.7	2

Christy Mathewson (1880-1925) was born and raised in Pennsylvania. He played on his first semi-pro team when he was 14 years old! Christy later went to college at Bucknell University where he served as class president and played on the school's football and baseball teams. He served in the U.S. Army and made his MLB debut July 17, 1900. He was one of the most dominant pitchers of all time and 1 of the first 5 into the HOF. 2x W.S. Champ, 2x Triple Crown, 4x wins, 5x ERA, 5x strikeout leader, MLB All-Century Team.

P
CY YOUNG

BEST SEASON STATS

1901	W-L	ERA	SO	SO P/9
	33 - 10	1.62	158	3.8

The "Cy Young Award" is given to the best pitchers in baseball every year. (AL & NL)

CAREER	PITCHED
1890-1911	906 GM

TEAM	HPY
RED SOX	$4 THOUSAND

WINS	LOSS	ERA
511	316	2.63

IP	SHO	SV
7356.0	76	17

SO	SOp/9	NH
2803	3.4	3

THE BEST

Cy Young (1867-1955) was born and raised in Ohio. He grew up in a small farming town and stopped going to school after the 6th grade so he could help out on the family farm. Cy played a lot of baseball as a child and joined his first semi-pro team in 1888. His MLB debut came on August 6, 1890 for the Cleveland Spiders (giving up only 3 hits in an 8 to 1 win). W.S. Champ, Triple Crown, 5x Wins, 2x ERA, 2x Strikeout. Cy Young holds many MLB records, including: most wins, innings pitched, games, and hitless innings.

1B/SS
ERNIE BANKS

BEST SEASON STATS

1958	AVG	HR	RBI
	.313	47	129

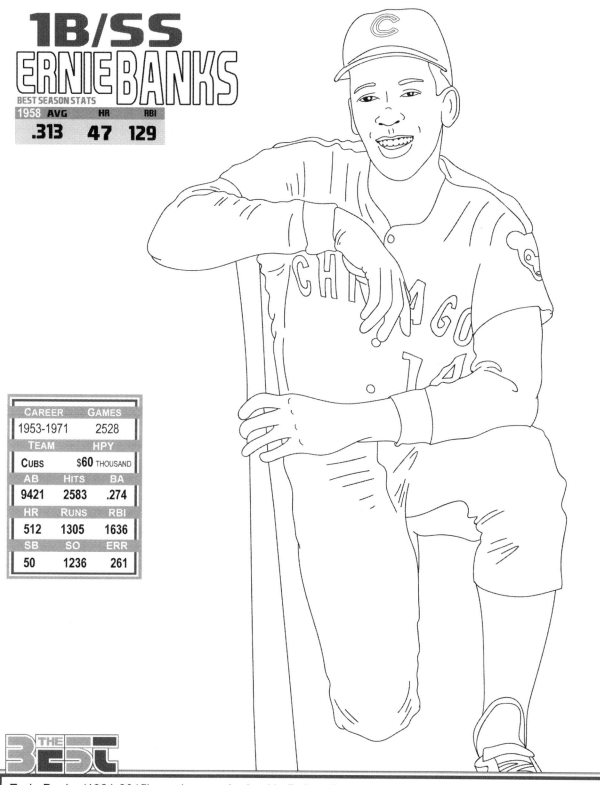

CAREER	GAMES
1953-1971	2528

TEAM	HPY
CUBS	$60 THOUSAND

AB	HITS	BA
9421	2583	.274

HR	RUNS	RBI
512	1305	1636

SB	SO	ERR
50	1236	261

THE BEST

Ernie Banks (1931-2015) was born and raised in Dallas, Texas. He had 11 brothers and sisters. In high school he was a star in football, basketball, baseball and track! In 1951, Ernie was drafted by the U.S. Army and fought in the Korean War. He also played basketball with the famous Harlem Globetrotters. In 1953, he signed with the Chicago Cubs and spent his entire career there. He was the Cubs first black player. 14x All-Star, 2x NL MVP, Gold Glove winner, 2x NL home run and RBI leader. All-Century team.

GREG MADDUX

P

BEST SEASON STATS

1995 W-L	ERA	SO	SO P/9
19 - 2	1.63	181	7.8

CAREER		PITCHED
1986-2008		744 GM
TEAM		HPY
BRAVES		$15 MILLION
WINS	LOSS	ERA
355	227	3.16
IP	SHO	SV
5008.1	35	0
SO	SOp/9	NH
3371	6.1	0

Greg Maddux (b. 1966) was born in Texas but spent much of his childhood in Spain, where his father was stationed while serving in the Air Force. Greg and his brother, Mike (4 years in the MLB) were trained by a former MLB scout. His brother was drafted in 1982 and Greg was drafted 2 years later by the Chicago Cubs. Greg went on to have an amazing career and became the first pitcher to ever with the Cy Young Award 4 straight years! 8x All-Star, W.S. Champ, 18x Gold Glove, 4x MLB ERA and 3x MLB wins leader!

RF
HANK AARON

BEST SEASON STATS

1971	AVG	HR	RBI
	.327	47	118

CAREER		GAMES
1954-1976		3298
TEAM		HPY
BRAVES		$240 THOUSAND
AB	HITS	BA
12364	3771	.305
HR	RUNS	RBI
755	2174	2297
SB	SO	ERR
240	1383	144

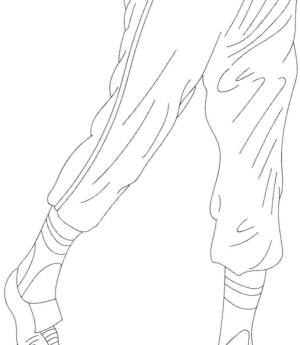

THE BEST

Hank Aaron (b. 1934) was born and raised in Mobile, Alabama. he had 7 siblings and one of his brothers, also played professional baseball. He grew up poor and he practiced hitting bottle caps with sticks. The Aaron's often created their own baseball equipment. Hank first played in the Negro American League, then in 1954 signed a contract with the Braves. A *25-time All-Star selection*! World Series Champ ('57), NL MVP ('57), 3x Gold Glove, 2x NL batting champ, 4x NL home run and RBI leader. MLB record, most RBI's!

2B
JACKIE ROBINSON

BEST SEASON STATS

1949	AVG	HR	RBI
	.342	16	124

CAREER		GAMES
1947-1956		1382
TEAM		HPY
DODGERS		$35 THOUSAND
AB	HITS	BA
4877	1518	.311
HR	RUNS	RBI
137	947	734
SB	SO	ERR
197	291	68

Jackie Robinson (1919-1972) was born in Georgia but moved to California with his family as a toddler. He grew up in a very poor and rough neighborhood, during a time when there was a lot of racial tension. Jackie played 5 sports in high school: basketball, baseball, track, football and tennis! In college, he was the quarterback on the football team and a superstar in baseball. In 1947, Robinson became the first black player to play in the MLB. 6x All-Star, W.S. Champ ('55), MVP ('49), batting champ, 2x SB leader!

15

CF
JOE DIMAGGIO

BEST SEASON STATS

1937	AVG	HR	RBI
	.346	46	167

CAREER		GAMES
1936-1951		1736
TEAM		**HPY**
YANKEES		$37 THOUSAND
AB	**HITS**	**BA**
6821	2214	.325
HR	**RUNS**	**RBI**
361	1390	1537
SB	**SO**	**ERR**
30	369	105

Joe DiMaggio (1914-1999) was born and raised in California. His father was a hard working fisherman and hoped that one day his five sons would also become fishermen, however 3 of them became major leaguers instead! Joe's legend began in 1936, playing for the New York Yankees (where he would spend his entire career). "Joltin' Joe" is perhaps best known for his 56-game hitting streak in 1941- a record that still stands! 13x All-Star, *9x World Series Championships*, 3x MVP, 2x batting, home run and RBI leader!

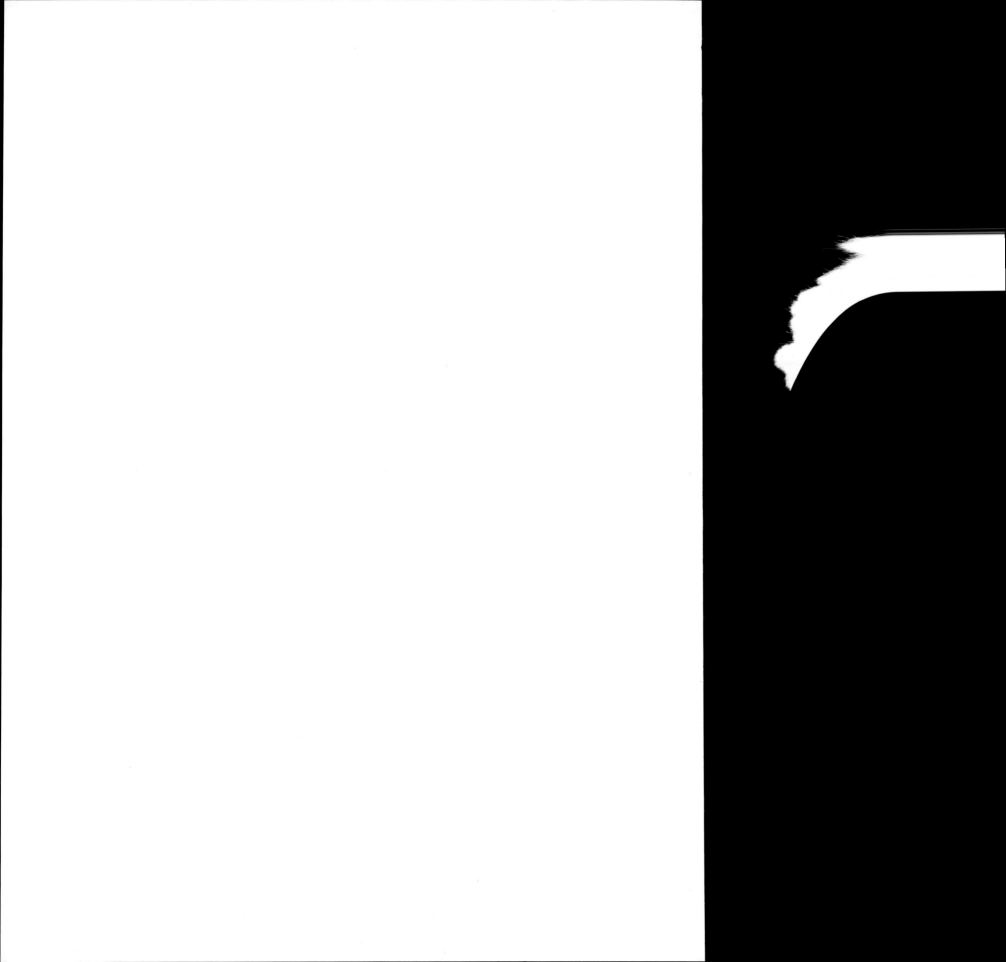

17

C
JOHNNY BENCH

BEST SEASON STATS

1970	AVG	HR	RBI
	.293	45	148

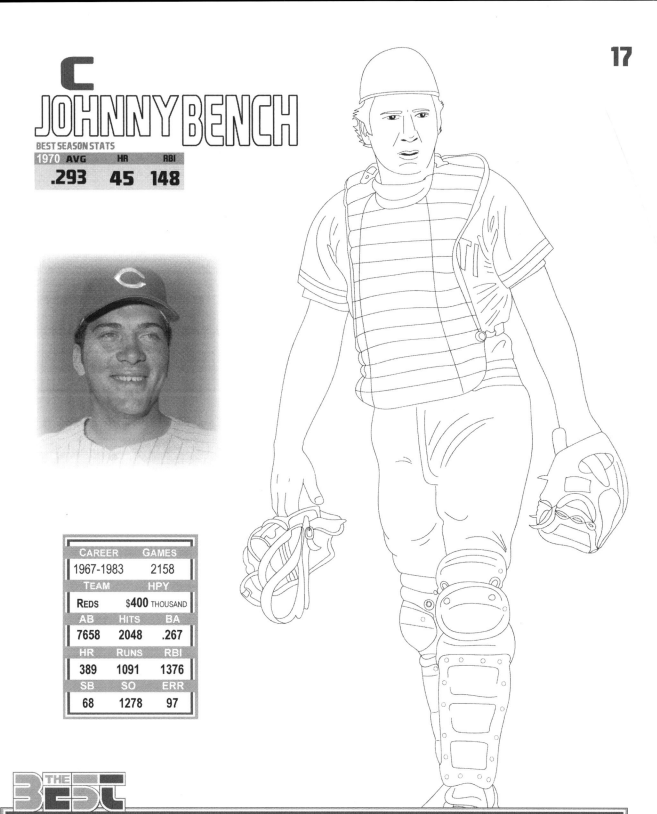

CAREER		GAMES
1967-1983		2158
TEAM		HPY
REDS		$400 THOUSAND
AB	HITS	BA
7658	2048	.267
HR	RUNS	RBI
389	1091	1376
SB	SO	ERR
68	1278	97

THE BEST

Johnny Bench (b. 1947) was born in Oklahoma and played baseball and basketball (and was also class valedictorian) at Binger-Oney High School in Binger, Oklahoma. He was drafted 36th overall by the Reds in the 1965 draft and played in the minor leagues for a few years. Johnny was called up to the majors because of his amazing defensive play. 14x All-Star, 2x World Series Champ, 2x MVP, Rookie of the Year, 10x Gold Glove, 2x home run and 3x RBI leader. ESPN called him the best catcher in baseball history!

18

CF
KEN GRIFFEY JR.

BEST SEASON STATS

1997	AVG	HR	RBI
	.304	56	147

CAREER		GAMES
1989-2010		2671
TEAM		HPY
MARINERS		$12.5 MILLION
AB	HITS	BA
9801	2781	.284
HR	RUNS	RBI
630	1662	1836
SB	SO	ERR
184	1779	89

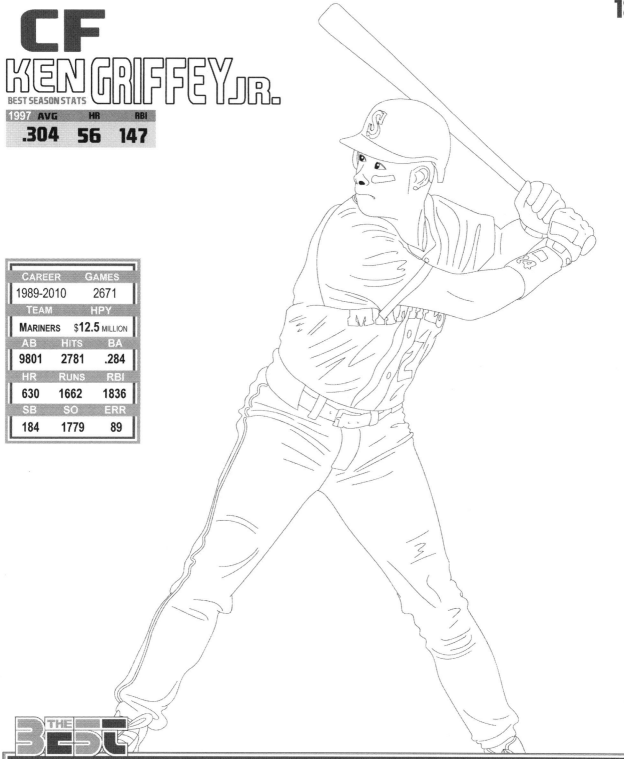

THE BEST

Ken Griffey Jr. (b. 1969) was born in Pennsylvania but grew up in Cincinnati, Ohio, where his dad, Ken Griffey Sr. played for the Reds. When "Junior" was 6 years old he was in the dugout during Ken Sr.'s back-to-back championships ('75/'76). A superstar at a young age, Junior was the number one pick by the Seattle Mariners in 1987. A 13-time All-Star, AL MVP ('97), 10-time Gold Glove Award winner, 7-time Silver Slugger, 4-time AL home run leader, Mariners retired jersey, Baseball Hall of Fame.

CAREER		GAMES
1923-1939		2164
TEAM		HPY
YANKEES		$39 THOUSAND
AB	HITS	BA
8001	2721	.340
HR	RUNS	RBI
493	1888	1995
SB	SO	ERR
102	790	193

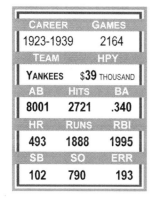

1B
LOUGEHRIG

BEST SEASON STATS

1927 AVG	HR	RBI
.373	47	175

Lou Gehrig (1903-1941) was born, raised, went to high school, played college baseball *and* professional baseball in New York City! Lou was an amazing athlete and went to Columbia University on a football scholarship but also played on the baseball team. He often played pitcher, striking out 17 batters in one game. However, Gehrig became a legendary hitter for the Yankees. 7x All-Star, 6x World Series Champ, 2x AL MVP, Triple Crown winner ('34), 3x home run and 5x RBI leader. Hit 4 home runs in 1 game!

MARIANO RIVERA

BEST SEASON STATS

2001	SAVES	ERA	SO	SO P/9
	43	1.38	80	9.2

CAREER		PITCHED
1995-2013		1115 GM
TEAM		HPY
YANKEES		$15 MILLION
WINS	LOSS	ERA
82	60	2.21
IP	SHO	SV
1283.2	n/a	652
SO	SOp/9	NH
1173	8.2	*1

*not recognized by MLB

THE BEST

Mariano Rivera (b. 1969) was born and raised in a poor fishing village in Panama. He played baseball and soccer with his friends, and his favorite athlete was soccer legend, Pele. They used milk cartons for gloves and tree branches for bats. Mariano later joined an amateaur baseball team, playing shortstop. He later was asked to pitch and quickly developed into one of the greatest relief pitchers of all time. 13x All-Star, 5x W.S. Champ, W.S. MVP, 5x Relief P.O.Y., 3x Delivery P.O.Y. 3x SV leader, MLB record for most saves!

1B
MARK MCGWIRE

BEST SEASON STATS

1998	AVG	HR	RBI
	.299	70	147

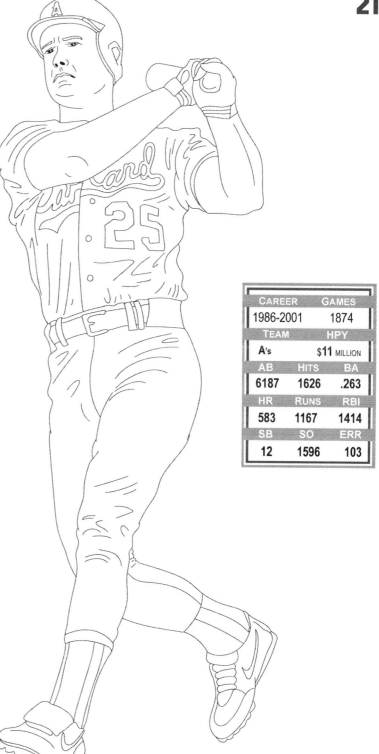

CAREER	GAMES
1986-2001	1874
TEAM	HPY
A's	$11 MILLION

AB	HITS	BA
6187	1626	.263
HR	RUNS	RBI
583	1167	1414
SB	SO	ERR
12	1596	103

Mark McGwire (b. 1963) was born and raised in California. In high school he played baseball, basketball and golf. He would go on to play college baseball at the University of Southern California (USC) and was teammates with future Hall of Famer, Randy Johnson! The Oakland A's picked McGwire 10th overall in the 1984 Draft. He was the AL Rookie of the Year, a 12x All-Star, 2x World Series Champion, Gold Glove winner, 3x Silver Slugger Awards, NL RBI leader, and *5x MLB home run leader!* MLB All-Century Team!

22

CF
MICKEY MANTLE

BEST SEASON STATS

1956	AVG	HR	RBI
	.353	52	130

CAREER	GAMES
1951-1968	2401

TEAM	HPY
YANKEES	$100 THOUSAND

AB	HITS	BA
8102	1677	.298

HR	RUNS	RBI
536	1677	1509

SB	SO	ERR
153	1710	82

In 2016, a 1952 Topps Mickey Mantle baseball card sold for $1,135,250!

Mickey Mantle (1931-1995) a.k.a. the "Mick" was born and raised in Oklahoma. He was an all-around athlete, playing both baseball and football in high school and was even offered a scholarship to play football at the University of Oklahoma! He was a switch-hitter (could bat both left and right handed) and made his MLB debut in 1951. He would become a legend and a hero to many. *A 20-time MLB All-Star!* 7x World Series Champ, 3x MVP, Triple Crown ('56), 4x home run leader. One of best to every play game.

23

3B
MIKE SCHMIDT

BEST SEASON STATS

1980	AVG	HR	RBI
	.286	48	121

CAREER	GAMES
1972-1989	2404

TEAM	HPY
PHILLIES	$2.25 MILLION

AB	HITS	BA
8352	2234	.267

HR	RUNS	RBI
548	1506	1595

SB	SO	ERR
174	1883	328

THE BEST

Mike Schmidt (b. 1949) was born and raised in Dayton, Ohio. After graduating high school, he went to Ohio University, leading them to the College World Series in 1970. He was named an All-American at the shortstop position. 30th overall pick in the 1971 MLB draft. Schmidt was one of the best athletes of his time and is often considered the greatest 3rd baseman in baseball history! 12x All-Star, W.S. Champ, 3x NL MVP, W.S. MVP, 10x Gold Glove, 6x Silver Slugger, *8x NL home run leader!* Hit 4 homers in 1 game!

24

P
NOLAN RYAN

BEST SEASON STATS

1973	W-L	ERA	SO	SO P/9
	21 - 16	2.87	383	10.6

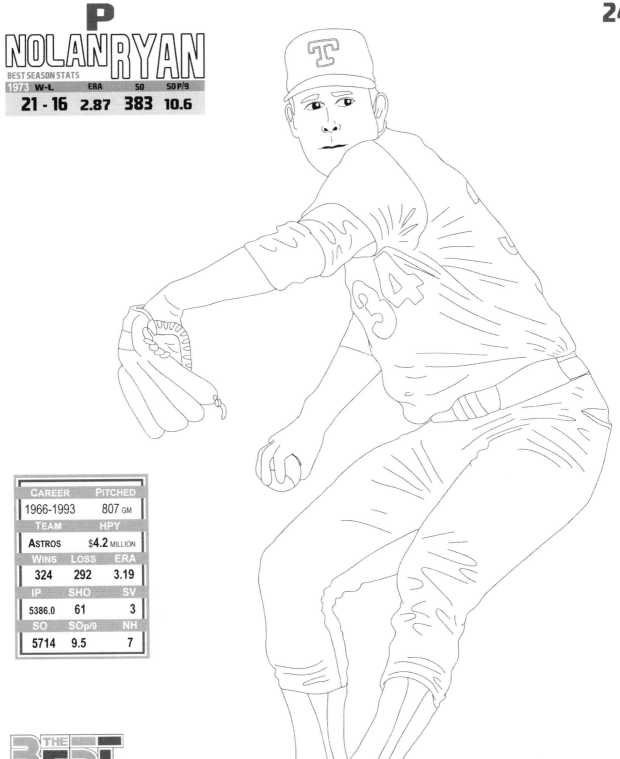

CAREER	PITCHED	
1966-1993	807 GM	
TEAM	**HPY**	
ASTROS	$4.2 MILLION	
WINS	LOSS	ERA
324	292	3.19
IP	SHO	SV
5386.0	61	3
SO	SOp/9	NH
5714	9.5	7

THE BEST

Nolan Ryan (b. 1947) was born and raised in Texas. He started little league baseball when he was 9 years old and made his first all-star team when he was 11. For 44 years, Nolan held his high school's record for striking out 21 hitters in a 7-inning game! In 1965, he was drafted in the 12th round by the New York Mets. Nolan regularly threw pitches over 100 mph and was known for a devastating curveball. 8x All-Star, W.S. champ, 2x ERA leader, *11x strikeout leader*, MLB records for most strikeouts and most no hitters!

25

PEDRO MARTINEZ

P

BEST SEASON STATS

1999	W-L	ERA	SO	SO P/9
	23 - 4	2.07	313	13.2

CAREER		PITCHED
1992-2009		476 GM
TEAM		**HPY**
RED SOX		$15 MILLION
WINS	**LOSS**	**ERA**
219	100	2.93
IP	**SHO**	**SV**
2827.1	17	3
SO	**SOp/9**	**NH**
3154	10.0	0

THE BEST

Pedro Martinez (b. 1971) was born and raised in the Dominican Republic. He had 5 other siblings and they lived in a small house with a tin roof and dirt floors. They did not have enough money for baseballs, so he and his older brother practiced pitching with oranges. His brother, Ramon, also played in the MLB. Pedro played a few years in the minor leagues, then was called up to the MLB. One of most dominating pitchers ever. 8x All-Star, W.S. Champ, *3x Cy Young*, Triple Crown, Wins leader, 5x ERA leader, 3x strikeout leader!

26

OF/IF
PETE ROSE

BEST SEASON STATS

1969	AVG	HR	RBI
	.348	16	82

CAREER	GAMES	
1963-1986	3562	
TEAM	HPY	
REDS	$1 MILLION	
AB	HITS	BA
14053	4256	.303
HR	RUNS	RBI
160	2165	1314
SB	SO	ERR
198	1143	213

Pete Rose (b. 1941), was born and raised in Cincinnati, Ohio. He played baseball and football in high school. While still in high school, Pete joined a AA team and batted .626 for the season! His uncle was a scout for the Red's and he was signed the following year. Pete's nickname was "Charlie Hustle" because he never quit, always played his hardest. 17x All-Star, 3x World Series Champ, NL MVP, W.S. MVP, NL Rookie of the Year, 2x Gold Glove, 3x Batting Champ, *All-time leader in hits*, games palyed and at-bats!

P
RANDYJOHNSON

BEST SEASON STATS

2001	W-L	ERA	SO	SO P/9
	21 - 6	2.49	372	13.4

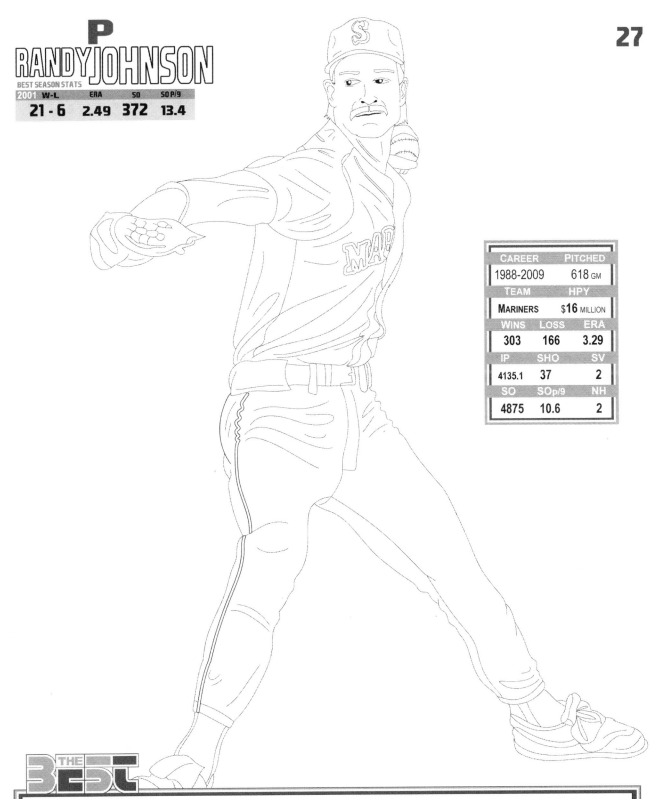

CAREER		PITCHED
1988-2009		618 GM
TEAM		HPY
MARINERS		$16 MILLION
WINS	LOSS	ERA
303	166	3.29
IP	SHO	SV
4135.1	37	2
SO	SOp/9	NH
4875	10.6	2

THE BEST

Randy Johnson (b. 1963) was born and raised in California. By the time he entered high school, Randy was a star in baseball and basketball. As a senior, he struck out 121 batters in 66 innings! He turned down an offer to go pro and instead went to USC, where he was a teammate of Mark McGwire. His nickname was "The Big Unit," being one of the tallest in MLB history at 6'10". One of the most dominating pitchers of all time. 10x All-Star, W.S. champ, 5x Cy Young, W.S. MVP, Triple Crown, 9x strikeout and 4x ERA leader!

LF
RICKEY HENDERSON

BEST SEASON STATS

1990	AVG	HR	RBI
	.325	28	61

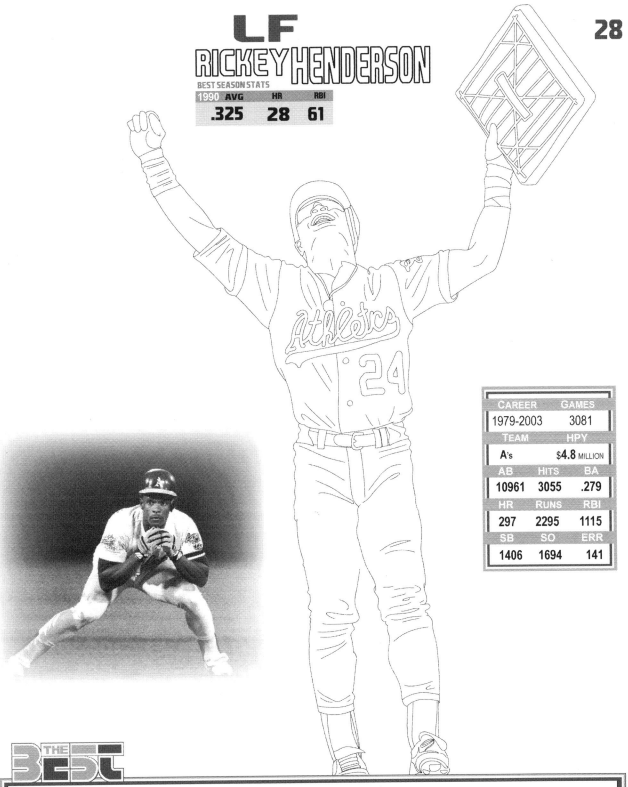

28

CAREER		GAMES
1979-2003		3081
TEAM		**HPY**
A's		$**4.8** MILLION
AB	**HITS**	**BA**
10961	3055	.279
HR	**RUNS**	**RBI**
297	2295	1115
SB	**SO**	**ERR**
1406	1694	141

THE BEST

Rickey Henderson (b. 1958) was born in Chicago but moved to Oakland when he was 2. While growing up he learned to bat right handed, even though he was left handed! In high school, Rickey played football, basketball and baseball. He was an All-American running back receiving many scholarship offers to play in college. His mother said "baseball players have longer careers," so he went with baseball! Considered greatest lead-off hitter ever. 10x All-Star, MVP, 12x Stolen Base Leader, records for most SB and Runs!

29

P
ROGER CLEMENS

BEST SEASON STATS

1997	W-L	ERA	SO	SOP/9
	21 - 7	2.05	292	10.0

CAREER		PITCHED
1984-2007		709 GM
TEAM		HPY
RED SOX		$18 MILLION
WINS	LOSS	ERA
354	184	3.12
IP	SHO	SV
4916.2	46	0
SO	SOp/9	NH
4672	8.6	0

Roger Clemens (b. 1962) was born in Ohio, but moved to Texas prior to high school. Growing up Roger played basketball, football and baseball. He was scouted during his senior year, but chose to go to college instead where he was a 2-time All-American at the University of Texas, compiling a 25-7 record. He was the 19th overall pick by the Red Sox in the 1983 draft. 11x All-Star, 2x W.S. Champ, 7x Cy Young, AL MVP, 2x Triple Crown winner, 4x MLB wins leader, 7x ERA leader, 5x strikeout leader. MLB All-Century Team!

30

2B
ROGERS HORNSBY

BEST SEASON STATS

1922	AVG	HR	RBI
	.401	42	152

CAREER		GAMES
1915-1937		2259
TEAM		HPY
CARDINALS		$40 THOUSAND
AB	HITS	BA
8173	2930	.358
HR	RUNS	RBI
301	1579	1584
SB	SO	ERR
135	679	307

Rogers Hornsby (1896-1963) was born and raised in Texas. He started playing baseball at a very young age. The first baseball team Rogers ever played on was for the meat packing company his brothers worked for. His older brother, Everett, was able to get Rogers a tryout for the minor league team he played for. In 1915, Hornsby made his MLB debut. He would soon become a legend. W.S. Champ, 2x NL MVP, 7x batting champ, 2x home run leader, 4x RBI leader, *2x Triple Crown* (lead in HR, RBI and batting AVG)!

31

P
SANDY KOUFAX
BEST SEASON STATS

1965 W-L	ERA	SO	SO P/9
26 - 8	2.04	382	10.2

CAREER		PITCHED
1955-1966		397 GM
TEAM		HPY
DODGERS		$125 THOUSAND
WINS	LOSS	ERA
165	87	2.76
IP	SHO	SV
2324.1	40	0
SO	SOp/9	NH
2396	9.3	3

Sandy Koufax (b. 1935) was born and raised in New York. He attended Lafayette High School in Brooklyn, where he was better known for basketball than baseball. He was 2nd in the league in scoring, averaging 16.5 points per game. He first started organized baseball when he was 15. Koufax later walked-on to the University of Cincinnati basketball team, then the baseball team! Soon, he was the star and the Dodgers took notice. 7x All-Star, 4x W.S. Champ, 3x Cy Young, 3x wins, 5x ERA, 4x strikeout and *3x Triple Crown!*

32

OF

STAN MUSIAL

BEST SEASON STATS

1948	AVG	HR	RBI
	.376	39	131

CAREER	GAMES	
1941-1963	3026	
TEAM	HPY	
CARDINALS	$75 THOUSAND	
AB	HITS	BA
10972	3630	.331
HR	RUNS	RBI
475	1949	1951
SB	SO	ERR
78	696	78

Stan Musial (1920-2013) was born and raised in Pennsylvania. He and his brother would play baseball with the neighborhood kids at an early age. Musial was a great all-around athlete, and was a star on his high school basketball and baseball teams. One of his teammates, was Ken Griffey Jr.'s grandfather! Stan was offered a basketball scholarship to play in college but chose baseball instead. Played all 22 seasons with Cardinals. *24x All-Star,* 3x W.S. Champ, 3x NL MVP, *7x NL Batting Champ*, 2x NL RBI leader.

33

LF
TED WILLIAMS

BEST SEASON STATS

1941	AVG	HR	RBI
	.406	37	120

CAREER	GAMES	
1939-1960	2292	
TEAM	HPY	
RED SOX	$90 THOUSAND	
AB	HITS	BA
7706	2654	.344
HR	RUNS	RBI
521	1798	1839
SB	SO	ERR
24	709	113

Ted Williams (1918-2002) was born and raised in San Diego, California. He was taught how to throw a baseball by his uncle, Saul Venzor, who had once pitched against Babe Ruth. After 4 years in the MLB, Ted had to serve 4 years in the Navy. Ted's goal was to have people point at him and say, "There goes Ted Williams, the greatest hitter who ever lived." He is regarded as one of the best, if not the best hitter to play. 19x All-Star, 2x MVP, 2x Triple Crown, 6x BA champ, 4x home run and RBI leader. Record .482 on-base %

CF
TY COBB

1911	AVG	HR	RBI
	.420	8	127

CAREER	GAMES
1905-1928	3034

TEAM	HPY
TIGERS	$50 THOUSAND

AB	HITS	BA
11434	4189	.366

HR	RUNS	RBI
117	2244	1944

SB	SO	ERR
897	680	278

Ty Cobb (1886-1961) was born and raised in Georgia. He grew up in a small town and his dad was a state Senator! Ty was fascinated with baseball when he was a kid. On August 30, 1905, Cobb made his major league debut, playing centerfield for the Tigers. He quickly became the star of his team, then the league, and forever will be a legend. One of the most aggressive players to ever play. *A 12-time batting champ!* 6x stolen bases leader. *Stole home 54 times in his career.* Holds record for highest career batting avg.

35

P
WALTER JOHNSON

BEST SEASON STATS

1913 W-L	ERA	SO	SO P/9
36 - 7	1.14	243	6.3

CAREER		PITCHED
1907-1927		802 GM
TEAM		HPY
SENATORS		$20 THOUSAND
WINS	LOSS	ERA
417	279	2.17
IP	SHO	SV
5914.1	110	34
SO	SOp/9	NH
3509	5.3	1

THE BEST

Walter Johnson (1887-1946) was born in Kansas and lived there until he was 14 years old, when his family moved to California. He spent most of his childhood riding horses, playing baseball and helping his father working in the oil fields. He later moved to Idaho, working for a telephone company while he played on a semi-pro team where he was noticed by an MLB scout. Walter soon became a legend. 2x MVP, 3x Triple Crown (W,SO,ERA), 6x wins and 5x ERA leader, 12x strikeout leader. MLB record 110 shutouts.

36

CF
WILLIEMAYS

BEST SEASON STATS

1955	AVG	HR	RBI
	.319	51	127

CAREER	GAMES	
1951-1973	2992	

TEAM	HPY	
GIANTS	$165 THOUSAND	

AB	HITS	BA
10881	3283	.302

HR	RUNS	RBI
660	2062	1903

SB	SO	ERR
338	1526	141

THE BEST

Willie Mays (b. 1931) was born and raised in Alabama. His dad, Cat Mays, was a talented baseball player and introduced the game to Willie when he was very young. In high school, he excelled in many sports, averaging (a then-record) 17 points a game in basketball. He was also the quarterback on the football team. Mays first played in the Negro leagues, then in 1951 made his MLB debut. Willie Mays is one of the best to ever play. 24x All-Star, W.S. champ, 2x MVP, 12x Gold Glove, BA champ, 4x Home Run and SB leader!

37

C

YOGI BERRA

BEST SEASON STATS

1950	AVG	HR	RBI
	.322	28	124

CAREER	GAMES	
1946-1965	2120	
TEAM	**HPY**	
YANKEES	$65 THOUSAND	
AB	**HITS**	**BA**
7555	2150	.285
HR	**RUNS**	**RBI**
358	1175	1430
SB	**SO**	**ERR**
30	414	125

THE BEST

Yogi Berra (1925-2015) was born and raised in St. Louis, Missouri. His parents were Italian immigrants and his father did not know what baseball was. "Yogi" is actually a nickname that he was given from a friend. His real name was Lorenzo Pietro Berra! Yogi played a year of minor league ball before serving in the U.S. Navy during World War II. In 1946 he played his first MLB game. Regarded as one of the best catchers in baseball history. 18x All-Star, *13x World Series Champ!* 3x AL MVP, All-Century Team!

3B
KRIS BRYANT
2016 SEASON STATS

AVG	HR	RBI
.292	39	102

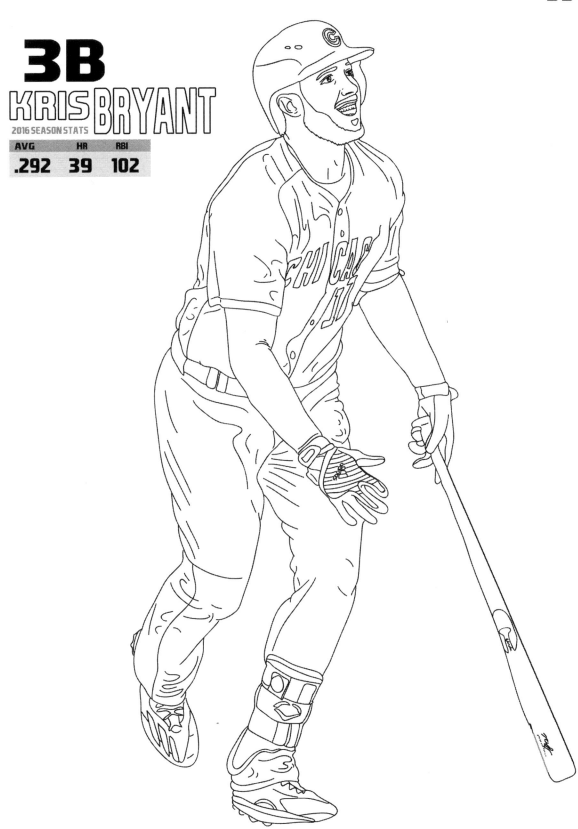

40

CF
MIKE TROUT

2016 SEASON STATS

AVG	HR	RBI
.315	29	100

41

SP
MAX SCHERZER

2016 SEASON STATS

ERA	W-L	SO
2.96	20 - 7	284

SP
CLAYTONKERSHAW

2016 SEASON STATS

ERA	W-L	SO
1.69	12 - 4	172

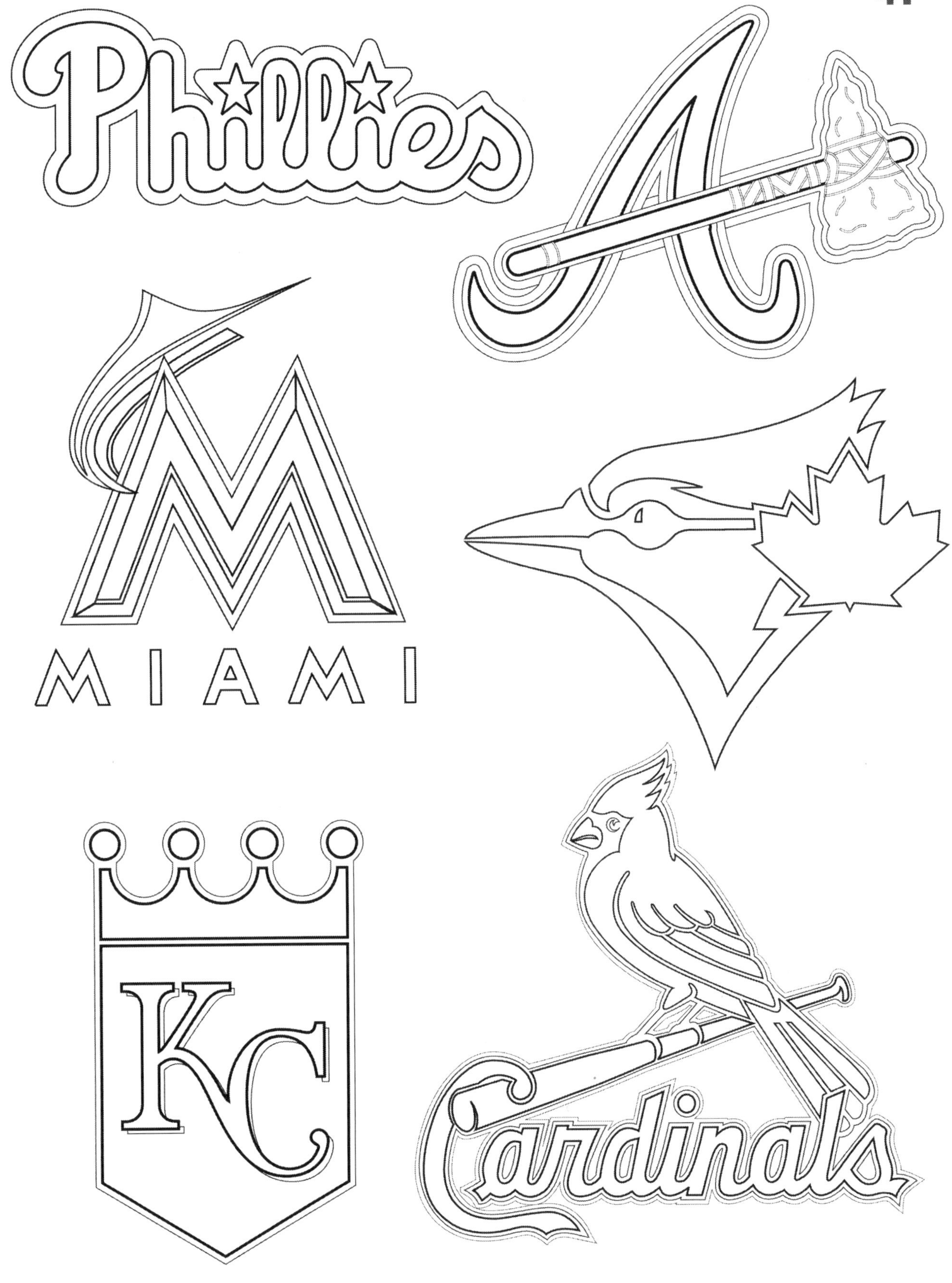
Phillies
MIAMI
KC
Cardinals

Made in the USA
San Bernardino, CA
29 November 2017